THE

POWER WITHIN POSITIVITY

THE
POWER WITHIN POSITIVITY

How to Apply it to Your Life

Richard McArthur

ISBN: 978-1-4269-8184-5 (sc)
ISBN: 978-1-4269-8185-2 (e)

Trafford rev. 08/01/2011

 www.trafford.com

North America & International
toll-free: 1 888 232 4444 (USA & Canada)
phone: 250 383 6864 ♦ fax: 812 355 4082

Introduction

"God is light and within it, there is no darkness"

This book was made with much love and thought. The ideas stated have been thought about and collected over the period of a year. When I started out my only motive was to make a book that would help in personal and global positive change. Within good time the book became so much more it became a guideline to living in a new state and a new positive/productive way. Many people will find that most of the ideas in this book ring a truth. My only wish is that people will pick up on this ringing vibration of truth and apply it to their lives.

I was at a very dark time in my life throughout the making of some of this book, a state of confusion, anger and depression. I had all of a sudden noticed that my negativity was tearing me away from the life of my dreams. For a good majority of time about a few months after beginning to write this book I had been kicked out of my dad's house where I was staying for being a party addict, a drug and alcohol addict and just somewhat of an idiot. My dad was disgusted with how I was living my life and the negative decisions that I was making. He thought that I wasn't taking my life serious enough, and he was right. All I wanted to do was to have a good time, but it was a path of destruction...I needed change.

I had then moved into my grandparent's house where things went smoothly for a bit until I got had got in with the wrong crowd of people. I began drinking and doing drugs heavy trying to relieve my pain and to discover myself but it didn't seem to work. My grandparents didn't appreciate that I broke all their rules and treated them with as much disrespect as I did. So they then kicked me out to sleep in their backyard on a couch where I got even more depressed and delved deeper into drugs and partying.

It was during these dark times that I discovered the power of positivity during some super high state "laughs". I was hopped up on all sorts of drug all the time and I began to have visions of a better life than I was living. My higher self was crying out for change and begging me to listen. So I asked my grandmother if she could find me a note pad and a pen and I began to write down my feelings. This led me into feeling happier about myself and somewhat cleaning up my act. But I knew there was so much more to what I was writing than there seemed.

Later down the road I was not accepted at my grandparent's house anymore because I told them off time after time; because I was sick of their rules. I was still blind from the powers of positivity and I still felt like a wreck so I became officially homeless and slept behind a dumpster and couch surfed for awhile until it truly hit me that I fucked up. I then began to look for work and I found it at a catering business which made me some money. Later I had hooked up with some friends and found a place to live with cheap rent fees. Things were starting to look up for me and ever since that point things haven't been all that bad.

We are at such a desperate time, and we are in desperate need of desperate measures. All I ask is that you read this book with an open mind and heart. Our lives always have room for positive change. No matter how dull and hopeless our lives ever seem there is hope. I am reaching out to all corners of the world, begging for change, begging for morality and order.

Those who believe in my movement will follow me and my word. Those who are foolish will stand in the shadow of the light and be blind of its power. Our people demand change, our freedoms, rights and ideas deserve to be voiced. When will our society, governments and citizens listen and learn? And is there any hope for our crumbling society?

Negativity is a game with no winners; it is a mental entrapment that keeps us locked from our higher purpose. Everyone has the right to be successful and live happy lives. We are all liable to self expression yet we are cut off from being able to properly getting heard and known. The government keeps us behind closed curtains of the bigger picture.

People are submerged in negativity, because we are conditioned to negative ways and realities. When we destroy that made up barrier of negativity, our eyes are open to the truth. The truth is that we are meant for more, we are meant to reach our higher positive potential. Don't be a slave to the government control, and don't be a slave to negativity of any form. You are so much more than what appears to be hidden when it has been there all along. When our souls get dusty with negativity, we must clean them and find hope within the heart of positivity. Open your eyes and see that the secret as well as the truth is being hidden from us and we are so stupefied by societies brainwashing to see it.

I 'am but one man, but together we are strong. We are all being controlled and conditioned by our governments and governing forces. There is no longer purity and personal freedom and room to grow. Our government holds us down and poisons us with a life of conditioning and control. Our land is free as we are born free, yet we are shackled and boxed in by our societies. It is important to see that not only are we being controlled and conditioned we are being tricked and lied to. The government loves to hide their secrets from us, they like to overpower us and play games with us like pawns on a chess board.

Our governments treat us like slaves, we work for them and there is this illusion that there is no freedom from our enslavement. They make it seem like everything is alright, therefore we submit to their systems of control and brainwashing. We have to realize that we are so much bigger than the conditioned lifestyle that we live. They treat us like mice in a maze of their control and power. We are expected to pay them, when they are the ones with all the money. The only way that we will break through their wall of lies and control is to fight back and to stand up for our personal and global rights and freedoms. Our governments are shallow minded and selfish by taking all control, when the control should be a joint effort; a "were all in this together" type of ordeal.

Why are we restricted from natural resources and opinions? Why are we limited on our freedoms? We should be free to explore self discovery of drugs without the government breathing down our backs afraid that we'll discover new dimensions of our minds and the universe. Why are we all conditioned to this shallow reality? The real truth is that we are being cut off from our land and resources. We are being cut off from opportunities, and we are being cut off from not only our physical freedoms but our mental and emotional freedoms as well.

This book is about our war against negativity and our overall detrimental problems. This book is about destroying this negative force that seems to run our nation and to replace it with a new consciousness a positive global movement. It starts with you, and it starts now. Meditate on the ideas in this book and take them to heart, and hear the cries of their truths. If this book changes the hearts, minds and souls of even one person then my job has made an impact. I hope that the world will listen and I hope that we will make it listen. I know that we are all sick of our diseased system and people; it's time to take a stand and to rebel. It's time to stand up for our rights, and freedoms it's time to be heard, and it's time to fight back (this time is now).

"Get up, stand up, stand up for you right, don't give up the fight"

-Bob Marley

Six Layers of Being
and Existence

Mind (computer)-Create, store and manipulate information.

Body/matter- Earth, universe, nature, and things.

Information-Mental information, physical
information, information in general.

Self, being/experiencer- Core aspect of self, individual,
independent, separate individual, and controller.

Emotions/feelings-Happy,sad,mad,scare
d,excited,sensual,anxious etc...

Senses-Touch,taste,smell,see, and hear.

"Blessed are those who hunger and thirst
for righteousness, for they will be filled"

Taking Control of Your Mind (computer) and Being the User

We must not become the information that is being processed by our brains; we must become the user or processer of that information. Therefore being able to more easily use our minds to our own success and desire. We can then create, sort, and manipulate information in any way we want.

When we are controllers of our minds instead of slaves we can easier use information. When we self program ourselves for success we attain it, because we program ourselves into becoming it. The more we push ourselves the better; all it takes is persistence, faith, and a personal need for positive gain. We must program ourselves in a positive way with positive skills and attributes.

The next step is to then use that information for our own good as well as the good of society and others. If we are using our information pointlessly, then what is the point of that information? So take control and don't lose yourself in the information you are creating or receiving, be the user, be in control, be yourself, and be your best.

When we are controllers of our minds instead of slaves we can easier use information. When we self program ourselves for success we attain it, because we program ourselves into becoming it. The more we push ourselves the better; all it takes is persistence, faith, and a personal need for positive gain. We must program ourselves in a positive way with positive skills and attributes. We must find our higher self and become one with it's glory.

"Strive for the best"

Being Yourself

What does it mean to truly be you? Well essentially to be yourself means to be who you want to be. We all create ourselves/personas, although it is very important to know who you want to be, therefore you know who to be. We should all think hard about what we want from life and ourselves, and strive towards that.

Take control of yourself and be yourself. Take control of your mind and your life. Once you have control, then it is possible for you to be the best you can be. This means being the thinker instead of the thinker's thoughts. Being the best you can be is what we all try to strive for, or at least what we should be striving for. When we are our best, look our best, and feel our best, we are more fulfilled as a person.

When we strive towards positive potential energy in our lives, we tend to spread that successful attitude to others. When people see you at your best, they often become jealous and want to be their best. When everyone is at their best, enlightened, happy and successful then there's no reason to be jealous anymore. Therefore take care of yourself, and take care of others and you will succeed in this life.

Be who you want to be and try to be the best you can be. Just stay focused, positive, keep your head up and you'll do fine. Strive for your dreams, reach for the stars, and don't settle for less. The more you practice the power of positivity in your life the better you will become.

"Life is good"

The importance of positive thinking, actions and emotions

The importance of positive thinking, actions and emotions is absolutely crucial. When we attach negativity to these three crucial areas, we are just asking for troubles and problems. Negativity not only brings us down, it brings down others and society as a whole.

When we bring about negativity, we degrade our higher potential influentially. Negativity is like rust as it grows things deter ate with it. Therefore for a better society, a better life, healthier friendships and a better more successful you, we all desperately need the power of positivity. We must be a generator of positive energy/ focus, not only for the betterment of ourselves, but for nature, things and others.

When we think, act and feel positive we have the attributes of a positive lifestyle and role model. If we seek a life of positive rewards we must first change ourselves to be compatible with those rewards. By becoming compatible with our higher purpose, we magically start seeing results. People pick up on our new lifestyle change and they may say something like, something seems different about you. What they don't know is that they too can have the life of their dreams if only they took my advice and teachings to heart. This isn't only a book it is a lifestyle change, as well as a change of heart that will change your life sufficiently.

"Live good"

Knowing that you are not your thoughts

Often times we tend to get caught up in our thoughts so much that we become entrapped in them. We must know that we are not our thoughts, and that we are free from their mental entrapment. When we are trapped in our thoughts, we tend to lose sight of ourselves. Although if we know that we are the person behind our thoughts, then we should never be lost.

We must know who we are and who we want to be so that we don't get lost and confused. Our scattered thoughts easily try to trick us into thinking were something that were not. On the other hand if we know who we are and who we want to be already then there is no confusion to deal with.

We can think all we want, but in truth we are the ones doing all the thinking. There are two levels to this idea "the thinker and the thoughts". The thinker is the being that is producing the thoughts. The thinker therefore should know who they are, so that they don't get mixed up, confused and lost in thought.

A person can think anything that they want, but that does not mean that those thoughts are the person. Try to know yourself or who you want to be/become as much as possible, so that you can live true to yourself. Don't always trust your thinking, because thoughts are deceiving, trust yourself and you'll be far better off. When we know ourselves we can be ourselves, and this leaves no confusion or second guessing. Know yourself, be yourself and don't let your thoughts take over, be in control.

"Try to make right decisions and learn from the bad ones"

Personal freedom

Personal freedom is the freedom of your beliefs, thoughts, dreams and desires. When you know that you have the freedom to believe, be and do what you want, you are then truly free. You have the freedom of choice, values, religion, beliefs and morals. You are the one with the choice, and the free will to choose. Your personal freedom is your choice, and is you're born right to personal decision making.

When we are truly free we act from our own best interest. Being free is a state of peace and inner harmony. So many people are so caught up in what's going on in their heads that they aren't fully present in the here and now. Our minds and thinking is the biggest cause of all of our problems. If we can be free from our thinking and most importantly negative thinking then we have changed our selves for the better in a huge way. Being free takes a lot of self discipline and control, but in the long or short run it is so worth the while.

Separate yourself from all else, singularize yourself completely. Be independent in your endeavors and free yourself from the jail cell of your mind. Instead of being a slave to your mind, make it your slave. Be enforcing full of your positive success and attitude, be the boss of yourself and mind. You can't let others tell you what to do all the time, and govern your life. You are the master of your destiny, the captain of your ship to success (so sail yourself in the right direction no matter what).

With positive thoughts, actions and emotions we are making "positive change with positive choice". If we use our personal freedom for positivity we'll personally succeed and become a role model for the success of others. Making your own decisions is the first step to success and life attainment. Making positive decisions is one of the main keys to success and life attainment.

"Think gain, live gain, know gain"

Being paid in positivity

Being paid in positivity means that positivity is a form of worth. When you are rich in positivity you are at your best and feeling your best. By being positive you are reaching towards your higher potential. When you are at a state of pure positivity, then you are no longer entrapped in stress and negativity. With our understanding of being paid in positivity we will soon see positive changes in our lives, and others will see it as well.

With a purely positive attitude we will be happier, friendlier, and will be more able to make positive choices for our betterment and success. Become rich with positivity and you will be more prone to fulfilling your dreams, desires, enjoying life, and feeling your best. There's nothing wrong with positive thinking, and that's the purpose of positive thinking; to erase the negative degrading energy that holds us back from our higher potential. Think positive, feel positive, live positive.

"No thought is better than a negative thought"

Living for love and fun

When you live for love and fun life becomes easy. It is no longer a challenge having fun, loving yourself, others and life. This great love brings purpose to your life and what you do, our lives become meaningful and we live for this meaning gratefully. You begin to live for a cause that is so meaningful, satisfying and easy that it just feels right. This kind of feeling is what we should feel because it is a good feeling. When we feel good because of love, joy, happiness and fun we are on top of our game and feeling great. We know that life is worth living, because of our love for life and the satisfaction we get from it.

Living for love and fun is so easy it's scary, just try it; the simplicity and satisfaction you'll get from it is endless. Open your heart to positive change and go with the positive flow. Enjoy life and its simple pleasures. Make moments last and cherish their magic and wonder one day at a time. When we live for love and fun we are happy and satisfied which allows us all to live a more successful, fulfilling life.

"Love life"

The essence of positivity, neutrality and negativity

Positivity is productivity, neutrality is permanence and negativity is deduction within the literature and confinements of this book. These three degrees of good, bad and in-between are what determines the course of our lives. How we use these polarities of power determine if we live a good life, a bad life or an average life, and it's all in how we deal with life, ourselves, others and situations.

Positivity is key in all our endeavors, because without it we slip into numerous problems. Our minds should be focused on positivity and positive aspects, but having a state of peace and neutrality is a good thing as well. Neutrality is a state of peace and harmony that blends nicely with a positive energy. When we achieve a neutrality of our minds combined with a positive mind state we not only achieve peace but enlightenment as well. Positivity is peaceful and it is tranquil and blissful.

When people send us negativity and we don't know how to react sometimes it is best to just shrug it off and keep positive. Other times it is necessary to fight back with negativity, but it is important to use your negativity for a positive cause. This theory is what I'd like to call an eye for an eye. Some people think that positivity is for sissies, but if it is to be used offensively as well as defensively it can be a weapon of great power. A person with a strong positive moral system is far stronger at heart and is more powerful than a negative minded/ hearted being.

If we live positively, think positively, act positively and feel positive then we'll be in greater touch with our higher productive potential. By focusing on the negative, we are trapped within a dark realm of our own stupidity. We degrade our higher potential, productivity and purpose by not aligning with our higher positive potential. Trying to reach our highest potential is a virtuous key to life and should be one of our main goals in our lifetime.

"Positive thoughts (mind) + positive actions+positive emotions= Positive results"

Connecting to the physical/body instead of mental for peace of mind

Connecting to physical properties is a great technique that allows you to obtain the peace of mind you seek. By shutting down our thoughts and simply being, we aren't focused on the mental aspects of being. We can then simply be ourselves, without a cluttered mind of confusion. Become solid in your mind and don't be so caught up in the air of your mind. Find positive, peaceful solidity and harness it into physical manifestation.

Our physical existence is at harmony and doesn't need an explanation or answers. Our mind is the hard drive that deals with information. With so much information it's hard to keep your peace of mind, but connecting to the physical/body is always a way to help, or even resolve the problem all together. Find your peace of mind outside of your mind because our minds tend to steer away from peace and get caught up in thought regularly. Try various things that work for you when it comes to peace of mind such as reading, music, meditation, hobbies, sleep etc...

"Live in your own positive enlightened bubble and don't let anyone pop it for the world"

Following the path of positivity and perfection

Following the path of positivity and perfection is a very precise path. To those who follow the path carefully, the rewards will be numerous. Staying positive will keep you focused and goal oriented, as well as happy and out of trouble. Positivity is the key to our personal success as well as our un-personal success. Perfection is the key to your ultimate attainment, as well as life and self perfection. Perfecting your life as well as your positive lifestyle is what will be the backbone of your overall success. Keep on the path of positivity and perfection, and you will be sure to see positive change. Alot of people may find the path hard to follow yet the the strong will prevail in its strength and glory.

"Our thinking/ beliefs creates our perceptive reality"

Positive programming and neural linguistic programming (NLP)

There is a developed skill and theory that exists that uses the power of mind control and mental programming. The theory states that by using certain thinking and subliminal programming (brain washing) you can obtain certain results. An example of this programming would be the use of powerful and positive successful thinking to achieve a certain task.

Our analytical or conscious mind is the part of our mind that analyzes, observes and deals with reasoning in everyday life. While our subconscious mind is the part of us that is creative and is open to suggestion and is more easily manipulated. Our subconscious is our higher creative selves and it is usually closed off to negative suggestions. Therefore if we can relax ourselves and perhaps play a tape with positive suggestions we would enter a state of positive self hypnosis. Our subconscious mind can be manipulated by suggestion. This technique can open our minds up to positive possibilities and even reprogram our minds for positive change and success in a very deep way.

If we had no motive, positive attitude or goal orientation where would we get in life? By using positive thinking and programming we can do almost anything. Our thinking greatly affects our results in many areas of life. If we were to rather think negatively and unsuccessful we'd become exactly that, because our thought determines our lives. You are what you think, if you think positive you will have positive productive results, and if you think negative you won't. Positive programming and NLP are great techniques to reach new dimensions of success, happiness, personal goals, dreams and desires. Ideas spark influence, when that spark appears turn it into positive, passionate fire and blow people away.

"If you aren't satisfied with what's inside, simply reprogram"

Becoming your own best friend, positive self talk, mental attitude and thinking

Getting yourself into a positive mental attitude is the first step to moving forward and succeeding in life. A person constructs their mental attitude on beliefs, self talk and the way they think. Track your thoughts, try to control your thoughts/mind and concentrate on the positive rather than the negative. If we can do this then we can gain a better understanding of ourselves and why we are like we are.

Every time you have a negative degrading thought it is best to somehow neutralize the thought or to replace it with a positive one instead. The key is to hack into your mind (computer) and program yourself for success and happiness using the power of positivity.

Our mind is like a garden and positive thoughts are like healthy thought vegetables, while negative thoughts are like nutrient robbing weeds. Therefore negativity is like a poison that poisons our higher potential. For the best results we should keep our garden healthy and well kept with positivity, love and care.

Try using positive self talk, thinking, emotions and attitude to obtain a harmonic state of bliss. Positive self talk is the art of using positive affirmations to obtain positive results by repeating them to yourself either mentally or verbally. We can change our feelings, beliefs, and aspects on life simply by changing our thinking. If we change our thinking for the better, with a little enthusiasm and action we can change our life dramatically for the better as well.

"Believe in yourself, or else you'll get nowhere"

Pure positivity

The art of pure positivity is really a test of will from an individual. People tend to get fed up with negative degrading energy robbing their positive productive potential. Why would you continue to let negativity continuously rob you of your own personal attainment and happiness? If you are sick of letting negativity bring you down then perhaps you'd like to try living a life of purity, a life of pure positivity and purpose.

Pure positivity will never let you down; make you feel bad, uncomfortable, unlikable or incapable. Pure positivity is knowing and having the confidence that you will not let negativity deter ate your life and potential. Reach for the stars with pure positivity, and stay true to its power, truth and cause. Pure positivity is your key to pure pleasure, happiness, success and attainment.

Positivity is my God it loves me; and it's knowledgeable, healing and generous. What more do we need from a religion, it is friendly and it is a guide to personal freedom, and success. Positivity teaches us to grow as people and to get over and beyond the hurdle of negativity. Positivity teaches us to perfect ourselves and to love and to teach and be a role model for others in a positive way. Positivity is our key to heaven on earth, in mind, in health, in heart and in our day to day lives. And it is real and it is tangible, while other religions and gods don't seem as much to be.

"Bath in the comfort, peace and warmth of positivity"

Positivity is purpose

Have you ever asked yourself why we do anything that we do? Why do we listen to our music, drive our cars, have our friends, play games, bother getting up in the morning, why do we date, watch TV or do anything for that matter? The answer to these questions is purpose; purpose is a little thing that makes a big difference. Purpose is good, because we all want it, so it must be good. We all want the good and don't want the bad yet people still remain confused. Some people think that they want the bad but they are simply delusional.

Positivity is our cause and it is our purpose. Live with purpose, don't live because you need to, be proud to live and have a purposeful life. Stay positive and you will naturally learn the purpose and joy of life. Life is like a game and you both enjoy and succeed in the game or you dislike the game and fail miserably for doing so.

Life is all about perception and polarity. If you think life sucks it will seem that way, but if you love and enjoy life it will seem very pleasant. The cup is either half full or half empty; the decision is ours to make. You choose how you perceive the world. If you see the world as a negative; hell it will become. Although if you think positively about life you will find joy and purpose in life and it will give you great strength to carry on. Positive perception is suggested to anyone who is looking for greater joy, happiness, success and purpose in their lives. The purpose of life is to gain enjoyment and positive outcomes from life's broad potential. "To change your perception for the better is to change your life for the better".

"Positive thinking leads to a positive encompassing outcome"

Making positivity your idol and or god

Positivity is simply a symbol that has deep meaning. A positive symbol has a special meaning to you for it is your key to enlightenment, contentment, satisfaction, and success. By making positivity your own personal idol and or god you are taking a big step into the world of positive thinking. With pure positivity on your side you become an extremely powerful being/character in the game of life. Pure positivity will never let you down it is your strength and absolute free will to greatness.

In order to live a positive and rewarding life we must be obedient to the higher power of positivity. Making Positivity your idol and or god is a huge step that asks for the release of negative tensions, and ways. For followers of positivity it is important to let positivity hail king over negativity and squash it like the bug it is. To empower people and change lives in a positive way is our cause. Try making positivity your idol and or god and see how it changes your life for the better. Positivity is the truth, it is the light, it is the way, and it is all powerful.

-People are encouraged to practice worship in anyway suitable, whether it be meditating, prayer, or simply just enjoying life.

"Positivity leads to more"

The power of having a positive attitude internally and exerting positive energy outwards externally

It is important to have a positive attitude and to be sure that your internal programming as well as your thoughts are positive. By having a positive internal system you are aligning yourself with a higher you, a higher potential, a better life and a more meaningful lifestyle. Having a positive attitude is the start of living righteously. A positive attitude mentally/internally is a great way to live life the way you want to and deserve to. Positive programming will erase your negative logic, theory, beliefs, thoughts, actions and overall aspect. Having a positive attitude is essential for success in any area of life; therefore it is of great importance.

The art of exerting positivity outwards is a precise skill. When you exert positivity you want to clear you negative motives and live with a new/fresh image of positive authority. By placing yourself in the authority of exerting yourself for a positive cause, you quickly find results in making friends, being social, relationships, hobbies, even your career. The key truly is positivity and the balance of how you exert your positive authority into your world and community.

Practice using your positive attitude in everyday life in order to obtain positive external results. By having your key of positivity internally, you will unlock your dreams and desires externally. Positivity is the key and exerting it into the world is the secret, now let it unlock the doors of your positive authority and personal positive freedom.

"Positivity is the key to solve almost every problem"

Awareness VS. Observation

Awareness- First of all it is important to know the difference between awareness and observation. They are both very important aspects of our realities. Awareness is simply being aware of your surroundings. Awareness is using your eyes and realizing what is around you as it is. The art of pure awareness is truly Zen, a state of clear consciousness and peace of mind without mental judgment.

Observation-Observation is the art of mental study, studying the essence and mechanics of everything. Observation is our own personal way to learn, to think and use logic. Sometimes our observation misguides us. When we learn to use our observation skills for our own good, then we are being truly productive in the way we run our lives personally. To observe is a necessary trick to gain knowledge and wisdom, in order to better ourselves as people. How you use your observation is up to you, it is a tool that can be used for good or bad, better or worse.

"Your inner self should always be positive towards itself, or else you would be your own enemy"

Having a positive outlook/perspective

If you have a positive outlook or perspective, then that view of things will become a reality. Positivity erases negativity; therefore positivity is your eraser which can erase your worries, stresses, problems and negative energy in any form. A positive outlook also requires a fresh perspective change. If you look at things and can see the good as well as the value of them then that's a good start. Life is all about absorbing worth out of its moments, as well as its wonders.

Having a positive aspect on life opens doors of positive possibility. We all have dreams, goals and desires, but if there is no real drive or intent then the possibility of achieving them is significantly lowered. Be positive and believe in yourself and your intents. Positivity makes a person feel better; think healthier, stay out of trouble and helps with making good decisions through your life.

We can keep a positive outlook/perspective by keeping a positive mind state, making good decisions and feeling happy. It is important to align ourselves with what we want in life, as well as whom we want to become. Stay positive, stay strong, and stay persistent. With a positive attitude, mindset and perspective, you will live like a champion, and will be victorious day to day.

"Positivity is the betterment of you and your life"

Becoming a universal self-model

To begin with we must clear everything away completely; pretend that you have a blank chalk board as a mind. This clear chalk board is the very center of your being, that talks, listens, understands, thinks, feels etc... Your mind is like the chalk that forms images, thoughts and ideas on the blank chalk board. Clear the board, and control the chalk. What is left should be a feeling of clarity/clear conception this is called peace of mind aka our essential being. We must then understand that we are the center of experience of the earth, the universe and all of existence.

Now here is another example of an individual's essential being. You are like a perfectly still body of water, and every emotion, thought, action or thing is a wave or ripple in the water. Your being is so pure that all else only taints it's purity. A good name for ones essential being would be consciousness of consciousness, "the conscious act of taping into and receiving continuous internal and external generated input/output". The self-model is a universal and earthly virtual simulation, "being you". You then begin to realize that at the very center and core of everything that we're basically the same thing. The only things that separate us are ego, personalization and misconception of self that usually occurs from ones strong tie to their ego.

Ones ego is not a great way to live because ones ego is too self-centered and closed minded and too separate. Every being is an individual clear-conscious controller that is constantly under a burden of internal and externally generated input due to a lack of understanding and conditioning. The main point of this section of the book is to help people understand that they are free beings, and that we have all the knowledge of the universe at the palm of our hands.

When you no longer become drained out in thought and emotions you are more yourself. You then have that free space to fill with happiness, love, pride and compassion. We must free ourselves from everything except for the peace of mind that stays true to our individual freedom. Erase everything from your mind and become yourself find your peace of mind and find your happiness within that peace and separate individuality. You are that perfectly still consciousness, when you become aware of it you begin to understand it, the only step left is to become it. The consciousness that has been all along looking for itself has been looking in all the wrong places, "for it is itself" free from everything for it is formless.

"Positivity is personal power at its max potential"

Living in the eternal now

The act of living presently in the eternal now would have to be inner alignment with the present moment. Once you align your mind and being with the moment you also align with the totality of life and the universe. This action tends to bring about a state of peace and oneness. When a person accepts being eternally here now, they then truly accept total control of their destiny, state of mind and emotions.

I like to call the eternal now the encompassing reality, the moment in which acts as a field on which the game of life is played. You finally become one with life when you become one with the now. This is a huge awakening for people and with great awakening comes great responsibility and compassion. Everything exists in a single moment called life, and we are all a part of its beauty and wonder. Align with the moment and live by it/for it; for it is where you're true self, your dreams and your enlightenment await. Be present, be aware, be here, and love the moment in which we experience and live the life of our dreams.

We all get so caught up in the world and all of its busyness. Our eyes are glued on the clock and we are enslaved by its existence. Time is only a measurement of the now as motion. The now is not moving, or being rushed it is simply at peace with the moment. If we seek peace and attainment we must come to peace and terms with ourselves in the all encompassing moment called now. As long as we deny this fact we will be lost in the world and enslaved by the hands of the clock. People need to realize that the now is real and that within it we can find our higher selves, purpose, enlightenment as well as peace.

"Put your troubles in the past"

Positive thinking

When it all comes down to it, staying and thinking positive usually never brings us trouble, stress or downfall. Positivity raises our awareness over an object or mainly a living being; it then wishes upon them the best of wishes and protection over their being and lives. If we treated everyone with this over ruling positive outlook there would be a lot less trouble in the world altogether.

Positivity, peace and protection will tend to never fail us if used properly; instead it will prosper our lives, the lives of others and the world as a whole. People find it so easy to bring others down because it makes them feel better about themselves, yet this is a very selfish way of thinking. What is so hard with peace, love, compassion and positive thinking? It's merely the separation, egos and stubbornness of people and society. When we lose this denial, separation, ego and stubbornness, we gain a feeling of love and oneness/completeness. We are all a part of this life and we all are legible to its joys and wonders. So think positive and live positive and you'll be sure to rise above negativity with compassion and love.

"Positive thinking will give you the power to change your life for the better"

How to create your own destiny

Once someone has accepted the totality of the moment, they must then accept to take care and control themselves in a positive manner. One should clear their head and align with their formless unchanged being which will be alert, responsive and ready for anything that comes its way. Another good point would be to act most importantly in your own best interest, as well as the interest of others. Some people act only in their own self-interest not thinking of others, even though others interact and have effects on our own personal lives.

To create your own destiny is to choose the energy, thoughts, words and actions to send out into the external world, and to do or say them as you wish. Align with the contentment and enlightenment with just being, as well as the totality of everything. Once you know what you are living for, you then have the correct passion to get started acting on it. Create your own destiny, leave your mark and enjoy the pleasure of being alive, self conscious and observant. You will always act in the moment and no other time but the moment, so harness the energy to act from its encompassing greatness.

"The grass is always greener on the positive side"

Living enlightenment and your highest potential

First an individual must realize enlightenment as their highest happiness, enjoyment, compassion and love. A person is best off to align with their higher self, which is their internal potential to reach their desired amount of self and life potential. In a lifetime it is best to be in control of your personal experience and highest potential. A real enlightened being already knows that were all the same in being and that our center of self (peace) is the pearl that experiences everything. There is nothing better than being alive as well as the controller and overseer of everything; therefore you truly are the best thing in existence being a human and all.

You are that number one spot, within this spot comes great confidence, compassion and personal freedom. Living enlightened is the personal decision to be happy, and to erase suffering, and to help spread that word in order to spread that cause. Enlightenment is identifying and aligning with universal love and compassion. Let the power and feeling of presence and happiness encompass your clear conscious being.

"You are only as great as you think you are"

Finding enlightenment in universal compassion

Enlightenment is the eternal inner fountain of contentment and happiness that comes with the totality of universal compassion. First one has to find compassion in the wonders and vastness of the universe and world. When we finally see that life truly is a magical mystery that were all a part of, we are then accepting our personal gift from life and the universe that everyone really wants. Once you understand happiness, compassion and positivity as the best method for the betterment of people and things, you then understand why personal and global enlightenment and positivity is so important. Enlightenment will affect everyone differently, although it's usually a feeling of great happiness, pride, oneness, love and compassion.

Think to yourself how you would like to feel if you had only a couple of minutes left on earth. Then imagine yourself crying and feeling sad or mad, and then think about how useless these feelings are to you. After you have imagined that next try imagining yourself happy and how good it feels to be alive and existing in such a great place experiencing life as such a great life form (human). This glorious feeling is the backbone of enlightenment and contentment with the eternal moment of being.

Our lives are a continuous model of our own brain structure. If we think we are mad at the moment we'll likely be mad, and if we think we're happy we'll likely be happy. If we think that were un-content then we'll likely feel un- content. Therefore what we think highly affects what we do as well as how we feel and act. If we think positively and strive to succeed, our chances of achieving our desired thoughts are highly increased. If we think negatively we'll be more receptive to failure and continuously fail until we change our thinking, feelings and actions.

Think to yourself in the present moment something that you want to do, then picture yourself achieving your desired thought and feeling good about it. Then think of what it takes to accomplish your goals and work towards them physically. If we use our minds in a positive way then we are more prone to physical manifestation and success.

Enlightenment means to bring a light of clarity, truth, happiness and meaning into your life. Every moment of every day is a test of our personal enlightenment. If we are not open to positive change and obtaining our dreams, desires and goals "now", then when will we be? There is no better time to discover your own happiness and positive/higher potential than right now. We must prepare ourselves to be able to do what we want to do, and enjoy doing it as well. Go ahead and accept your dreams, your true/higher self, and accept your own personal right to enjoy your own life to the fullest. To those people who seek to find enlightenment through themselves as well as through universal compassion this book is for you, for that is one of its main suggestions.

"Our lives are only as great as we make them and see/ visualize them"

How everything is manipulated by our minds

Many people have very little grasp of self, they don't know their essential being to be emptiness or clear consciousness, all they know is the things that they attach themselves to. These kinds of people have little control, and likely have a mind full of clutter and confusion. They think they are anything but nothingness, so they try to find themselves in everything else, yet they continuously fail to. When a person does not understand their true being they tend to become lost in a frenzy of thoughts, and emotions that they think to be themselves. When we get lost in our thoughts and emotions we become a mere projection of what is going on inside ourselves. We always have to talk about our problems and we get absorbed in our own egos, because it's all we know to be real. These kinds of people become lost of true peace and condemned to a life of utter chaos, for they never really seem to shut their minds up because they never really figure themselves out.

The self exists in a realm of timelessness and formlessness therefore it is separate from all form and is entirely independent within itself. Our minds and egos are continuously perceiving, deceiving, judging and or manipulating a number of things. To find true peace of mind we must see things as they are; unaffected by our own personal deception. A car is a car, a dog is a dog, and a thought is a thought these things are not you and they are existent independently. Things are not your thoughts of them they are what they are, and you are what you are, together we are it. Don't let your mind confuse the truth, and try to use your perception in a positive way so that you see the world through a positive lens being your own personal perception. Our perception of the world is our personal right, but how we choose to use it is up to us (choose wisely).

"Make it all good inside"

Rational and realistic thinking

Thinking rationally is the art of accepting reality and proper reasoning. Rational thinking is usually the foundation of a well educated person, a realist and someone who is good at reasoning and decision making. A person who uses rational and realistic thinking can much easier see truth in their reasoning/decision making and how they perceive reality. Reality is what it is, yet often times our perception can twist the truth profoundly.

We are all observers, yet it is not fair to judge people and things by how they look or how they may have acted. Someone may have been a trouble maker at one point in time and the next their good people. The people that are aware of their true nature and have their peace of mind and happiness are usually much more tolerable than someone lost in their own egos and problems. We all perceive the world around us, yet we must remember that it is always changing therefore our judgments can sometimes be extremely conditioned and judgmental.

Through our true being we will be more receptive to positive energy because we are at peace with ourselves and all of life. With great peace can come great joy as well as great realization of the bigger picture. It is important to remember that our world is of a neutral existence by itself, we are the ones that bring all the joy, happiness and love into the world. Our perception of the world is strictly personal, and we should make the best of it. We are the ones that bring about suffering, death, hatred and violence to our glorious gift being the world and the life we live in it. To change ourselves for the better is to change the world for the better. Think rationally/realistically and you will be more able to approach and work towards your goals as well as earning a clearer view of our mixed up realities.

"Let your positive being shine to its max potential without fear, for fear is negative"

Thinking of ourselves in a dream like perspective

Keep in mind the 6 layers of being and existence-physical, emotional, mental, awareness (self), senses, and information.

In a dream perspective we find ourselves outside of our physical bodies and inside of a mental projection of ourselves. This point of view is a great way to perceive ourselves and the world around us. When we are dreaming our brain tends to relax and slowly wash away the clutter of our minds, which aligns us with our true selves being peace of mind and subconscious self development. When we have that peace of mind we can function at a higher level with a clearer head and perspective.

There are a few important levels that make up the constructs of our being. There is the physical level which consists of body, conditioning and being. Then there is the emotional level which can be very fluctuant in an array of feelings and moods. Our emotions are a tool that can be either our own best friend or our own worst enemy. Everyone's emotions are different; some people tend to feed of negative emotions, while others feed of positive ones. Your emotions are yours and you are responsible for your own emotional state. You can enjoy yourself and have a good time or you could drown yourself in your own misery, stress, un- satisfaction and self pity. Since it is much better and productive feeling positive, confident and happy these positive states of emotion are highly suggested. Don't let negative emotions bring you down, stay cool, happy, present and under control.

The next level is the mental level this is where all of your thinking, imagining and problem solving are done. This is the level where you make decisions for yourself, as well as learn and process information. All information comes from either internal or external sources; our minds then store/ remember certain information or images. This level only correlates to the mind and intelligent beings with personalities of their own.

Next is the awareness/self level which is a form of mental peace and stability. When our minds become still at peace and observant, we are more attentive to what is happening in the external world around us, instead of what is floating around inside our heads. Our minds can become cluttered with useless junk, and can sometimes steer us away from a clear receptive perspective. If our minds are tainted; often times our sense of reality and attentiveness can become tainted as well. Often times it is best to have a good sense of peace of mind and to be very aware, because if we didn't we could miss out on a lot of opportunities. Don't let your mind control you, and distort or mix up your reality, stay focused and alert and you will be much more receptive to success.

"All levels correlate together to form reality, the world/universe and our own personal experience."If we can master and understand all levels of our beings and our existence, then we truly become masters of ourselves and the world all around us.

"Knowledge of positivity= awakening to higher purpose"

Stepping up to the plate and putting your dreams into action

Stepping up to the plate means having the drive and ingredients you need to live out your dreams and become the person you'd like to be. It also means being ready to take on challenges, and certain hurdles that stand in your way. Stepping up to the plate is the first step in living out the life you want and deserve, besides learning and planning.

Planning is an important factor in order to obtain personal success, because without a plan to work towards there is nothing to work towards. There cannot be any proper work towards something if it hasn't been properly planned and or thought about. It is important to do your homework and to have the necessary information in order to properly work towards a certain dream or desire.

This is why schooling is so important in life because without any knowledge of anything, these things become nearly useless to us. Knowledge is power, and without knowledge we are weak minded and dumbfounded by what to do.

Make plans to achieve your dreams, desires and goals so that you know how to succeed properly. Planning must be done carefully and should be delved into deeply. Planning or plotting will lay out the blue print of your success and is often a very important process. Don't be lazy when it comes to planning or else you may not be properly ready for your success. After you are done learning and planning for your success in a particular field you are then likely to be ready to begin putting your dreams into action.

 Putting your dreams into action means following through with accurate plans so that you can physically achieve them. Planning, plotting and learning are all mental levels of fulfilling your dreams and desires. The next step after mental preparation is physical preparation and or action. First you must learn and plan for what you want or want to get done, then you must endure it and make it a reality. When we see all of our dreams, desires and goals in this simple view we'll be able to begin working towards them as so.

"Hate and fight negativity for it is our biggest enemy"

Clearing your mind, becoming more focused and avoiding rumination and stress

Have you ever found yourself reflecting on your problems, and stress? Are you constantly bringing up negative things about your life into conversation? Well it is a fact that dwelling on negativity and stress tends to only cause more stress. Although we can learn from our problems by reflecting upon them which is a positive thing. Learning from problems is natural and healthy, but dwelling on negativity and stress isn't. Stress and rumination are harmful to your physical, mental and emotional well being.

When we keep our minds dwelled upon stressful situations of the past were in turn robbed of our joy in the present moment. It is better to learn your lesson, let go and move on. Clear your mind and let go off the things bothering you, let everything go and become the clear conscious controller that you were made to be.

The faster we can clear our minds of negative tension, the faster we can get back to peace of mind and enjoying ourselves/ lives. Know that you are in control, and not your inner dialogue. The time to be in control of your mind, life and destiny is now.

Here are some techniques in relieving stress, obtaining focus, control and peace of mind:

-a nap   -reading   -talking to someone (conversation)   -take a walk

-exercise   -music   -yoga/meditation   -a hobby

When it comes to clearing your mind and increasing your focus it's really up to you how you handle that task. Try a few techniques from the list above or just try anything you think may work for you. Your mind is personal and how you choose to clear it is just as personal.

"Don't let negativity bring you down, get lifted with positive uprising"

The difference between vision and perception

Our eyes enable us to see a usually clear and stable image of our external world. While our minds create judgments and personal perceptive thoughts from which we see. There are two layers to our experience there is the act of just looking and seeing, and then there is a layer of mental perceptiveness behind that layer. When it comes to vision everything is equal, except for appearance. Up until the point where we begin to evaluate, observe, judge and perceive the world around us everything is just, even and neutral.

The way that we perceive is all of the difference, for it is what we believe or think of an object, person or thing. If we perceive things as negative then those thoughts ring true to our belief system of those things. If we perceive things as positive then those thoughts ring true to our belief system.

Everybody perceives a little differently, so we must be open to new optimism and the perception of others as well. What we may think of something may be different or even opposite of what another person may think or perceive. For example a certain girl may think that a certain guy is attractive while another girl will think he is unappealing and ugly. It is important that we try to see the best in everything and have a positive perceptive thinking structure. How you perceive things affects how you experience life, so use your powers of perception to your own good.

"Become one with your higher potential"

Becoming somebody who understands and gets life (common sense)

Once you become somebody who gets and understands life, life then becomes much easier. Life is all about structure and common sense, like 2+2=4 or that a wheel rolls because it is circular. Once we become smart in our life endeavors, we will be able to live with less stress and confusion. When we use our common sense we align with the natural intelligence of the earth. If we simplify life and use our common sense we will be much better off. So try using your common sense on a regular basis and watch as it instantly simplifies your life, instead of living your life in confusion and unnecessary complication.

"Simplify life"

Cleaning the window of your perception with positivity

Our perception is our outlook of the world from our internal stand point. We use our perception on a daily basis, but if we have a negative or wrong perception then cleaning is likely needed. A negative or unclear perception is nothing but trouble. Having a foggy perception is like having fogged up glasses and you won't be able to properly see where you're going or headed.

The process of cleaning our perception is similar to cleaning a window or anything for that matter. We rid of the old dirty messy clutter in our minds; in trade for a clean/clear perspective and perception. Having a clean/ clear perspective and perception allows us to understand things better, achieve peace of mind and be more successful. With a clear mind and a positive outlook on life we are able to live a happier more successful life as well as a more peacefully one.

"Live free and abundant in positivity"

Positive transformative visualization

Positive visualization is the art of using the power of our minds to achieve a positive transformative state. We truly are living a virtual simulation/ visualization of our lives. We are constantly aware of our inner beings thoughts and surroundings. It is ourselves that control our destinies; we are the only ones that have control over our actions, moods and emotions. When you see life as positive your negativity melts away. Without negativity our problems are all of a sudden solved, our stress relieved and the weight of the physical world is off our shoulders.

Your positive visualization is the total of your experience; you create your experience with your own thinking. Life is what you make of it, so make the best of it with a positive vision. Stay positive, enjoy life and don't sweat the small stuff. Positivity will bring you a life of meaning and joy. Inner happiness and positivity are some main keys to personal success. Our positive mind set will bring us positive abundance. Positivity will protect you, direct you, help you, heal you and transform you.

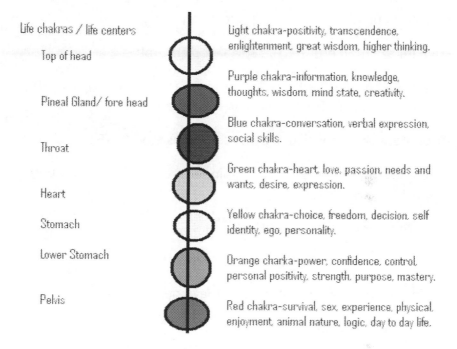

Life chakras / life centers

Top of head

Pineal Gland/ fore head

Throat

Heart

Stomach

Lower Stomach

Pelvis

Light chakra-positivity, transcendence, enlightenment, great wisdom, higher thinking.

Purple chakra-information, knowledge, thoughts, wisdom, mind state, creativity.

Blue chakra-conversation, verbal expression, social skills.

Green chakra-heart, love, passion, needs and wants, desire, expression.

Yellow chakra-choice, freedom, decision, self identity, ego, personality.

Orange charka-power, confidence, control, personal positivity, strength, purpose, mastery.

Red chakra-survival, sex, experience, physical enjoyment, animal nature, logic, day to day life.

<u>Rules of thumb for a positive/ rewarding life</u>

-A positive and confident mind state   -Be happy

-Positive thoughts   -Live with meaning

-Positive perspective on life   -Don't live in fear

-Think success and strive for success   -Be independent

-Become personally positive (positive self singularity)   -Be a free thinker

-Love yourself   -Do what makes you happy

-Balance your life chakras/ centers   -Strive for victory

-Align with your higher self and thinking   -Try your hardest

-Perfect yourself and life   -Handle negativity

-Live for the moment   -Be social and enjoyable

-Think positive and healthy about your future   -Try to be healthy and positive about your body   -Be brave

-Work towards a positive and enriching lifestyle   -Be persistent

-Seek and find your eternal happiness, personal enlightenment, and pure enjoyment

-Be strong hearted and persistent

-Be confident in yourself and in your success

-Be in control not your thoughts, achieve peace of mind

-Be the best you can be

-Love life

"With a positive and confident mind state you can achieve almost anything"

Having a positive emotional status

We all go through a wide variety of emotions on a daily basis. There are three kinds of emotions; positive emotions, negative emotions or no emotions. Positive emotions allow us to have a positive good feeling while negative emotions cause us to have a negative degrading feeling, while having no emotions leaves us in between. When we use our emotions in a positive way, we then feel on top of the world and at our best. With negative emotions we feel low and we deter ate our positive rewarding potential.

Sometimes it seems hard to stay positive mentally and emotionally when something negative has happened. Although fighting the urge to think negatively or make yourself feel bad is a better/smarter idea. When we feel good we are able to work and function properly as well as gain success and respect in life. By feeling good we attract good things to happen and when we feel bad we attract bad things to happen. By thinking and feeling good we align ourselves with our higher potential, and we begin to live a more positive and rewarding life.

"You are the one who controls how you feel"

What we dwell upon we become

If you apply productive, positive and perfecting qualities to your being and mind that is what you will become. Positivity directs us through inner peace and healing. Inner peace enjoys positive company so much that it begins to transform itself in accordance to it. What we seek and dwell upon we become if we seek or dwell upon anger we become angry; if we seek and dwell upon happiness we will become happy. The key to being is direction; we are either working towards our own good or against it. We can be our own best friends or our own worst enemies; the choice is ours to dwell upon.

"Our minds are full of deceptions, we must clear our state of deception and awaken to what is, and then we must awaken to the greatness of what is"

Positive affirmations

Affirmations are things that we think or say to our selves constantly that affect our own personal success and behaviors in a positive or negative way. Using positive thinking and affirmations is the art of using positive thoughts and sayings to gear our minds for success and positive attainment. Positive affirmations can change our moods, beliefs, and inner truths for the better. Here is a list of positive affirmations for positive changes that you can think, say, read or play to yourself daily.

-I can change   -I can be happy   -I can handle my own problems

-I can be a winner   -I can be cool   -I can fit in   -I can be original

-I can accomplish anything I set my mind too   -I am great

-I am confident   -I can let go of fear   -I am positive   -I am strong

-I can control myself   -I can be assertive   -I can make friends

-I can move on   -I can be prosperous   -I can be wealthy   -I love myself

-I can public speak   -I am a leader   -I am creative   -I can succeed

-I can achieve peace of mind   -I can be a good friend   -I am responsible

-I can be funny   -I can be a good at conversations   -I belong

-I am intelligent   -I can beat my addictions if I wish   -I can do it

-I can achieve my dreams, desires and goals   -I can make friends

"If you want to change yourself or the world change you're thinking"

Positive and negative cycles

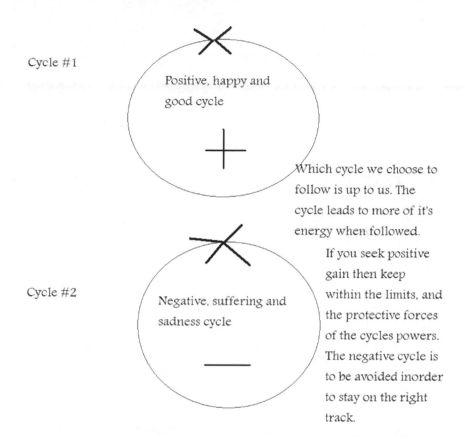

Cycle #1

Positive, happy and
good cycle

Which cycle we choose to follow is up to us. The cycle leads to more of it's energy when followed.

Cycle #2

Negative, suffering and
sadness cycle

If you seek positive gain then keep within the limits, and the protective forces of the cycles powers. The negative cycle is to be avoided inorder to stay on the right track.

The cycles tend to repeat and manipulate the particular energy being generated. Each cycle has karma based principles, because most of the time energy tends to copy itself. Positivity leads to more positivity while negativity leads to more negativity.

"Stay strong, stay positive"

Order and universal law / karma and karmatic effects

- Love over hate

- Good over bad

- Positive over negative

- Happiness over unhappiness

- Confidence over un- confidence

- Success over failure

- Etc...

Universal laws:

-Our material world runs on universal law, order and karma/ karmatic effects.

-Our mind and body run on universal law, order and karma/ karmatic effects.

-If bad is to be used it should be used for good either personal and or in-personal.

-If hate is to be used it should be used for good either personal and or in-personal.

-If negativity is to be used it should be used for a positive cause either personal and or in-personal.

-If unhappiness is to be used it should be used for a greater grasp or realization of happiness.

-The soul of a person or being is the controller (the animator).

-Learn from your failure to further your success, but do not strive for failure unless that's what you wish to obtain.

-If one is not faithful to their masculinity or femininity they shall suffer for their stupidity.

-We create our realities with our thinking, perception, beliefs and actions.

-Positivity over negativity

"What you plant is what you shall harvest"

The positive and negative magnet

-Negativity is devaluing and will lower your personal gain and in-personal gain within good time.

-Positivity is full of value and will raise your personal and in-personal gain.

Devalue   (-)   (+)   value

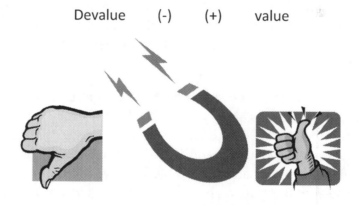

"It feels better to win than to lose"

Positive awakening

There are many ways to attain enlightenment yet there is only a few ways of achieving it properly, adequately and fully. When you awaken to the light of positive strength and healing; that strength and healing enter your being. When you receive that strength and healing you feel strong and new because you are erased from negative tensions and distractions. Negativity tries to distract us from our positive potential. Negativity is our worst enemy it will always try to fight against us. Positivity is our sword and shield to protect us as we fight off negative energy in all forms.

When we understand that positivity and goodness is the very thing that we all strive for, this is when we begin to awaken. Like the eyes after sleep open; slowly but surely opening to the light of possibility and the world each morning. Our hearts will begin to slowly grow with a burning fire of love, happiness and peace. We must find our inner peace through happiness and independent collective connected individuality. We must open our minds and hearts to an endless wave of peace and love that fills our beings infinitely.

To awaken means to awaken your heart, soul (self), body and mind. To awaken all of your senses and stimulations until you obtain an epiphany that transforms your life into greatness. A great realization is like a puzzle when the puzzle is put together you can clearly see the big picture. It takes a person a lot of time, thinking, studying and meditating to figure out the puzzle of life, years or perhaps a lifetime.

Enlightenment is the art of lightening the weight of the world and everyday life. Happiness and wisdom don't come easily to everyone; one must meditate on the art of happiness and wisdom for much time until they truly know it and feel it. One must transcend space, time and all of matter and spread his love and happiness outward in order to accept the love and joy of all else. To love is to connect; the more you love something the more connected you become. Love what is right for you, be a free thinker, be your own best friend and be independent. Enlightenment is an independent choice to love yourself and the world around you on a very deep connected level.

"Once you replace negative thoughts with positive ones, you'll start having positive results." ~ Willie Nelson

Becoming Lucid

Lucidity is a state of pure awareness and control. To become lucid you must align with pure awareness as well as absolute control of yourself and your surroundings. For someone who gains absolute lucidity, they then gain a higher state of wakefulness and are less absorbed in their thoughts. We must awaken to the truth of life and reality as a whole. Too many people are caught up in their own delusional realities and thoughts that they don't see the bigger picture. Our perceptions are like windows that we can only clearly see through when they are in absolutely cleared of all mental dirt and clutter.

When we dream there is a state of mental awareness called lucid dreaming where one can control their dream selves as well as their surroundings. If a person can perfect lucidity in the dream state as well as their waking state they can truly grasp the idea of the pure awareness of the lucid state. To achieve a state of pure lucidity one must obtain great wisdom, peace of mind, and must be very observant and aware. You are control, you are awareness, you are the master of your reality, now you must act like it (become one with truth).

"Live the dream!"

Inner and outer enlightenment/ happiness

Inner enlightenment is the art of self discipline, worth and happiness. When a person begins to experience inner enlightenment they gain a positive personal boost along with a state of bliss, happiness and healing. Every being whether they know it or not have not only a want but a need for inner enlightenment. Personal enlightenment and happiness is so drastically important, because without personal happiness/enlightenment we are truly lost. Without personal happiness we cannot truly grasp the concept of outer enlightenment and happiness.

Enlightenment is a state of selflessness, a state of pure bliss and a state of self attainment/ love that spreads through you into the world if you let it. We must free our minds completely and liberate ourselves in a state of pure sense and observation. When our minds are truly free we can live more independently and we can focus on what is truly important to us. Our thoughts are independent from us, we watch them pass by but they are not the being watching them. We are the controllers of our destiny; we must accept the happiness and enlightenment that we want/seek. If we seek peace of mind then we must gain control over our thoughts, and if we seek attainment then we must attain it within the moment. We must hold tightly to the moment and all it's got to offer and we must also show it what we have to offer in return.

Outer enlightenment is different than inner enlightenment because it is enlightenment within the outer limits of ourselves. Happiness is found not only within a person but without a person. One must find happiness around them, if they wish to see happiness around them. Happiness is all around us it just takes an open and joyful mind to truly see it. Our enlightenment lies in how receptive we are to it, if we are receptive to happiness it will be found in even the most unexpected places. Smell happiness, taste happiness, feel happiness, see happiness, but most of all be happiness.

"Happiness is within us, as well as all around us just open up and welcome it into your heart, mind and soul."

Left and right brain (Conscious/analytical and subconscious)

Left brain (conscious/analytical) traits: Logic, language, Science and math, reality based, order and pattern, practical, sequential, factual, analytical, awake, reasoning, doubts, fact, beliefs, conscious.

Right brain traits (subconscious): Intuitive, Creative, art and music, fantasy, imagination, random, feeling, symbols and images, sleep, relaxed, crosses borders of reality and realism, open to most suggestion except negative suggestion in most cases, subconscious.

(Physical)   (True being/awareness/consciousness)   (Mental)

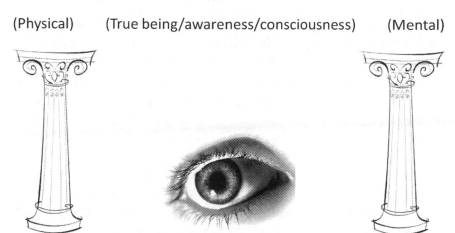

"Add positivity to all these fields of self and nature"

How to feel good all the time (embrace positivity and feeling good)

If we seek to feel good all the time we must truly grasp the concept of a positive state of mind, emotion and lifestyle. The more we embrace the power of positivity and happiness the more we can understand its nature. By understanding the benefits we are more receptive to taking advantage of those benefits. We must immerse our heart, minds and souls into the purifying lake of pure positivity and goodness. A mass overload of positivity will heal our negative energy and turn it into pure positive energy. This state of positive purity is the exact state we must achieve to be truly happy and feel good all the time.

This state of pure bliss and ecstasy is what the ancients have been talking and been preaching about for so many years. A state of ultimate attainment and self perfection is only as easy to achieve as you let it be. The day we accept the truth that positivity will reign supreme over negativity is the day that we awaken to a higher state of consciousness. This higher state is what the entire world needs to wake up to and put into action immediately.

All our suffering is due to a lack of positive action and belief. Our government lacks the positive motivation to fulfill the needs of its people. We are entrapped in a system of far too much negative power and closed mindedness. Our rights are taken from our own personal freedoms as people. We are born free and we live in a land of freedom. All people are liable to enjoy their lives to their max potential, yet we live in a system of confinement and torture.

The people are restricted by laws, money and a government that seems to care little for its people. We are all enslaved by the almighty dollar, we are all enslaved by our system, and we are all obliged to conform. What kind of life have we created for ourselves? What kind of trap have we put ourselves into? And where has our freedom gone? If we had any dignity for ourselves and our future as a nation we'd rise against our collective negative tendencies.

It is a new century, a new age and we demand positive change and healing. I cannot stress enough how important positivity is and the impact it has the potential to make. Forget about all the negative forces that you've known for so long and just let it go for it is less than nothing. Negativity will destroy us, and it will destroy our planet and culture. Instead focus on growing in the light of positivity and illuminate this knowledge and higher power to others. Be a role model for the world to look up to, to respect and acknowledge. Leave a positive mark on the land that we so desperately need and love. Love the collective dream of life and embrace its greatness. Strive for the best, and don't be afraid to feel good in a world that tends to get us down, because of negative tendencies. Shine to your max positive potential and step on the negative scum energy of our society. Hold your head up high, and walk with pride for you know the truth and you know the unifying productive power of positivity.

"Overflow the cup of your soul with the essence of immense positive power"

Charge yourself with positive energy (meditation and visualization)

Positive charge opening the light chakra technique

Steps:

- Sit in a comfortable relaxing environment with some quiet relaxing music or just in silence.

- Take a few deep breaths and let your mind and body settle and relax.

- Now imagine all of your chakras in their correct order within your body or soul.

- Next imagine that a very bright radiant sun is your light chakra just above your head.

- Imagine that this sun is all the good, loving, peaceful, happy, positive energy of the universe.

- Let this energy of the sun become your light chakra.

- Feel its radiance fill your being as it runs down your lower chakras starting from your third eye chakra down.

- Let the light of this pure positive sun divide itself into its divine full spectrum as it fills each chakra with pure positive energy correlating to each chakra and colour.

- Feel the immense healing that this energy is applying to every aspect and attribute of each correlating chakra.

- After you are done this continue to sit in meditation and imagine your chakras glowing with pure positive radiance at their max potential. Bask in the glory of this feeling and soak up the happiness that comes with it. (You are that sun and all of its shine).

The light and the light switch technique

Steps:

- Sit in a comfortable relaxing environment with some quiet relaxing music or just in silence.

- Take a few deep breaths and let your mind and body settle and relax.

- Think of a light and a light switch then imagine how drowned out and dull everything appears to be in the dark.

- Next imagine that this dullness is a symbol of your life, and the world around you. This darkness is a symbol of individual and collective negativity.

- Now see that this type of thing is not only unproductive but wrong all together.

- Understand that this change must be answered.

- Imagine a light switch, then imagine flicking it on.

- Instantaneously each beam of light will represent the collective awakening of positive change and higher conscious awareness and meaning.

- Now imagine the room full of this pure and positive healing light.

- Then imagine just what kind of immense change that it is capable of.

- Become the change that you seek to obtain.

In with the good out with the bad

Steps:

- Sit in a comfortable relaxing environment with some quiet relaxing music or just in silence.

- Take a few deep breaths and let your mind and body settle and relax.

- Once you are relaxed imagine that every time you breathe in you are breathing in positive energy and good things.

- Hold this positive energy into your being and let it collect within your very soul/ being.

- Then breathe out slowly and imagine that when you do this that you are releasing all of your negative energy, worries and stresses.

- Fully empty out your lungs of all that negative energy.

- Keep repeating until you feel renewed and full of positive energy and feelings.

"Relax, renew, restore and reconstruct"

Positive manifestation and positive mental reprogramming

Positive manifestation is the ability to create and manifest positive things into our lives. When we program our minds with a perception of pure positive consciousness, we can then properly manifest our dream lives into realities. When we harmonize with our higher energy then we harmonize with our higher selves and lives. We all vibrate at a certain frequency within areas of our beings, and we all have an energy field. When we have a positive overall state of ourselves and our chakras, we give out a positive vibe because we carry a positive charge. Positive vibes come from positive states charges and consciousness. If we seek to change the world, we must change ourselves in every aspect.

The more aspects we perfect with positive beliefs, the more we become the image of perfection. Creating a perfect state of consciousness is how we control everything else. How we are constructed is how our actions will be constructed. If we have troubles dealing with our own positive gain, we must be crazy. Yet this law is still being broken over and over. Why do we keep falling into holes that we keep digging? When will we see the light atop the hole, in which we keep slipping into? This is the global question of this century for me? Why must we keep on this low vibrating negative frequency as a whole? And as a nation!

This is the era of a new conscious awareness, a global awareness. Why must our young be convicted for living their lives? We all learn, and we all make mistakes. There is other ways of working things out than throwing them in a cell, taking their money and mistreating them profoundly. Perhaps one could work their payment off for the victim or pay them back themselves etc... There is a long list of better ways to resolve problems than to restrict people to years of probation, strict regulated laws, and charges. Why must we sink ourselves so low as to create such a hateful society? Why do we run a society of homelessness and unemployment, and financial bankruptcy? Are we not perfect enough one comes to ask? And to boot were all supposedly supposed to die in 2012... Who's responsible for our sickening lives and society? And why are our freedoms caged? Why, why, why?

All of our questions are being unquestioned, and our ideas are not being properly exploited. A select few run the world, a so called higher authority due to some unexplainable reason. The people must be listened to; our ideas need to be heard. How will we grow to our higher potential while were being held back. When it comes to war everyone gets signed up without question, yet when we try to voice our opinions no one listens. We all stay so closed minded to our higher purpose that it's sickening. Why mustn't we treat all like family? Why must we hate? But most importantly why do we bring these kinds of things about ourselves?

Is our world being run by some demonic power? Why is there so much controversy about satanic or occult presidents, famous and government officials? Why are we confined from this, why is the public hidden from the fact that these people are not setting a very positive role model to the world on which it runs. If you don't believe me look it up on the internet (it has been said that many people in power are involved in secret societies). We demand peace, we demand freedom, we demand respect, and we demand our dreams. WE WANT ANSWERS AND WE WANT THEM NOW!

Imagine if the world did end 2012 or any time soon all the people in jail cells and poor situations and conditions that can't live out their dream lives. Is the world so heartless to let its people suffer? For African countries to be suffering when we are limited to money and job options. So many are turned down for work because they aren't clean or don't own nice clothes or don't fix their preference. Yet this judgment becomes a letdown for people and they start to lose self esteem when they continuously get turned down. People are expected to be able to pay for years of schooling and a number of other expenses rent, food, clothes, utilities etc... Yet the majority of us are being underpaid. With so much taxes and deductions and low pay how are we supposed and expected to live. How are we expected to provide for our children, and our children's children? Where is all this money appearing from?

What we need is a global conscious shift an awakening into a new collective consciousness that nurtures our lives into positive productive blossom. We must work together as a hill of ants and help to provide for the entire hill with all the ants (people) helping to provide for the collective. There is a massive amount of people that are coming to notice that there's a desperate need for positive change. We know that we need to change our ways, yet we still haven't sprung into action. This new thinking must be publicized, and put into action as soon as possible. This kind of thinking and action will be the building blocks of our new and brighter lives. A new global awakening, and a new era for our freedoms and rights to be put first. A world of positive encouraging influence, more global offers, less problems and less worries/ stress. We must change as a nation, we must change as people and we must change for all the right reasons.

The day that a global wakeup call is put into order is the day that we truly wake up. This is our call, and this is our right; this is our world. We should be willing to change for the collective best interest. Will we ever see the changes we seek? It does seem right now that probably not I know, yet it must be. The faster the better, although proper planning time is necessary of course. People must start voicing their ideas, preaching their beliefs, and a global movement must rise up above our impurities. There must be a worldwide purification, a world of hope for a greater today as well as a greater future.

"Positive thoughts are the foundation for positive change and results"

Rules of positivism-

- Try and do good internally as much as possible.

- Try and do good externally as much as possible.

- Stay true to Positivity for it is your friend.

- Stay clear from negativity for it is your enemy.

- Positivism can be applied to most current religions/ God can be seen as positivity.

- To fight against negative forces, for positive reasoning.

- Follow positive and productive teachings.

- To become a role model and teacher for others.

- Make positivity your idol and/ or god.

Replacing negative thoughts with positive ones

Everyday our minds are continuously thinking yet it is proven that many of us are consumed by negative thoughts. Some people even think negatively more than they think positively. Why do we let ourselves get brought down by our own thinking? Our thoughts create our realities and perceptions on the world. Without positive thinking we are weak minded and weak spirited.

I encourage my readers to simply replace their old negative ways with a new way of thinking; a positive way of thinking, resulting in a positive lifestyle. It is easy to get things tangled up and confused within the confinement of our minds. The key is to not let anything bring you down, but to stay up in the clouds where you are safe from all the negative forces of the world.

Whenever you find yourself thinking of a negative thought simply switch it with a positive thought of your choice (or no thought even). Let's say you had a thought saying that you couldn't get a job because you were too lazy, instead think "I can get a job and I am more than ready to work and be hired for work". When we reprogram our thinking for our success that is what we will obtain. Our minds are like machines, we must program a machine to run how we'd like it to. If we program the machine of our minds to fail it will fail, and if we program it to succeed it will likely succeed.

The key is to program your own success. You are in control of your own success, you are in control of your mind and you are in control of your destiny. Take control for yourself and focus on yourself first of all. In order to become number one we must be firm and focus on looking out for number one aka ourselves. Put yourself first; focus on you and perfecting yourself in all areas. Keep a positive mind and don't let negative thoughts break you down. Remember to replace your negative thoughts/ thinking with positive thoughts/ thinking. After repeated practice of this theory your negative thoughts will start to disappear all in all, or at least be replaced.

"Practice makes perfect"

Positivity in the 6Layers of being and existence

-Mind (computer): Positive programming. Positive, successful, confident, and productive mind state/ attitude. Master your mind. Become more positive and focused. Be goal oriented. Be in control of your mind and thoughts. Create positive thoughts. Create positive actions through positive thinking/ thoughts. Relieve stress and relax. Have a clear and positive perception. Learn from experience. Learn from your chakras.

-Body/matter: Engage in physical, and mental health. Respect your body. Treat your body like a temple. Become a positive vessel. Be filled with the light, love and happiness of pure positivity. Enjoy the physical aspects of life and or spiritual aspects of life. Love your body. Find your image and style. Be comfortable in your own skin. Love the world, the universe and all of its wonders. Love nature and the joys of nature. See positivity through nature. Learn from negative nature or natural disasters.

- Information: Strive to become intelligent and wise. Understand information and its purpose and cause. Higher intelligence. Know your mind and how it works. Use information in a positive and productive way. Be higher than intelligence (be yourself). Be creative, self expressive. Be a free thinker. Use information to your advantage. Learn from information. Learn from your chakras.

-Self, being/experience: Be yourself, find yourself, know yourself, know what you like, know and follow your beliefs. Don't have self doubts. Be confident in yourself. Live free, but safe. Be your best. Be positive. Follow and love a positive lifestyle. Treat yourself well. Enjoy yourself and life. Create a good and positive life for yourself. Have a positive self image. Be the experience and love the experience. Make the best of life and yourself. Live your dreams. Strive for your dreams and reach for your goals. Be successful. Be in control. Don't let information and your thoughts control you and misguide you. Be your higher self/ true self. Be independent and a free thinker. Heal and charge your chakras.

- Emotions/feelings: Become more enlightened and happy. Don't let people and the worries of the world hold you back from you potential to be happy. Find inner peace. Accept positivity as your god and let it fill your being with its essence and energy. Relieve stress. Meditate, and visualize. Do what makes you happy. Enjoy the senses. Learn from negative emotions. Heal and charge your chakras.

"Perfect positivity"

Positive and negative interactions

Positive interactions:

Positive interactions occur when one person sends the other person some form of positive interaction.

Examples:

-Positive and productive conversation

-Complements

-Good jokes

-Positive jesters

- Being fun and exciting

-Expressing love and gratitude

-Respect

-Confidence

-Be a good friend

-Be generous and outgoing

-Be friendly

-Be loving and self respective

Negative interactions:

Negative interactions occur when one person sends the other person some form of negative interaction.

Examples:

- Unnecessary violence

-Hatred

-Name calling

-Putting someone down

-Ignorance

-Racism

-Disrespect

-Negative conversation

-Negative jesters

-Lack of confidence

"Avoid negative interaction, and thrive with positive interaction"

The importance of being a positive role model/ leader

People are easily influenced by others. This means that the way we act will be likely to have a either positive or negative effect on others. By setting a positive example we can change the views of others. Once a person can grasp the idea of positive gain and its manifesting power, it is then easier to be influenced. Positivity is a hypnotic attracting force that will not let us down if used correctly. We've all been looking for a way out of our worries and negative restrictions, what's holding us back "the truth is out and free". We must grab our tickets to a positive paradise and fly away free from our negativity as soon as possible.

When we understand the truth and the secret of life and the universe, then it soon clicks in that we must embrace this theory. When people pick up on our positive attitude they will likely either join in happily or else they will fight back with negativity. Some people are so negative that they deny the truth of positive nature. We have been taught that rebelling and being negative is cool, therefore it has been accepted. The truth is that a righteous person that is true, stern and enjoyable is so much cooler than someone who's negative all the time. When we feel good about ourselves, and our lives other people pick up on that and join in on its greatness and glory.

We must set an example for our youth, for our people and for our future. If we continue to let our youth be brainwashed by negativity, how will they grow up? And how will they grow positively? Why is it that there are killers, bullies, racists, addicts, and homeless? Is there more to the picture than meets the average eye? People are obviously being influenced by negativity of many forms, and it's even being done under the nose of our collective societies. Why must we continue to spread this destructive action and energy into our world and the minds that live within it? When will we stop and look at what kind of influence we are creating for our people and society? When we awaken to our own stupidity, we can then correct that stupidity with positive intelligence and action. Just remember that the only people that can really change the world are the people that want to and strive to.

"One stone can have a big impact on a body of water, as one person can have a big impact on society and the world"

Removing self doubt

The first step to removing self doubt is to recognize your self-doubt and to understand that it is only degrading your potential. If we seek to reach new heights as individuals we must take action and control for our own lives. Educate yourself and become involved in self improvement other than self destruction. If we have nothing but self doubts we are bound to fall into repetitive downfalls. Our own belief in ourselves is one of the biggest most important things that we can do. Understanding this noble truth is the beginning of self transformation.

Identify with your bad habits and thinking and change it, anyway you can. If we don't change our ways from negative to positive we will never see the bigger picture of our higher potential. We must have confidence in our decisions, because our decisions are what create our fate. First we must stop blaming and start acting. The more positive we are about our success and ourselves the better off we will be.

We must put a stop to our self sabotage all in all, and take a stand for ourselves. If we don't hold our ground who will? The truth is it's a doggy dog world and it's everyman for himself. No one can change our lives like we can. It is easy to blame our doubts on others and situations, but the fact of the matter is that we are in control of our outcomes. We are only as good as we think we are, so stop doubting yourself and reach for the top. Exchange your thoughts of self doubt for ones of self confidence. The more we believe in ourselves the higher the chance we will succeed and this is a proven fact. Quit keeping yourself back find inner and outer positivity and fly free to your higher limitless potential.

"Self doubt equals self pity"

Looking out for number one

By looking out for ourselves and our own success we are looking out for number one. The day we believe that we are number one, is the day we gain our self confidence. By loving ourselves we teach others to do the same and act as a good role model. Strive for the best and you will align with the number one spot. To be the best we must think, and act like the best. If we want the best life possible for ourselves we must strongly encourage ourselves to strive for the best in all areas of our lives and selves. This kind of action and discipline may take awhile to fully comprehend and obtain, but it's more than worth the work and wait.

Lift yourselves higher than you could imagine, and don't be afraid because positivity will guide us in a positive forward direction. Have faith in your beliefs and faith. Have hope that you will succeed and enjoy the rewards that come with it; for there are many. If we were all to think in this way and strive for the best that we can be then we would all be much better off than we ever have been. This kind of action takes courage and self strength. I know some people are scared that they cannot succeed due to some form of reasoning or fear, but that's all bullshit. Forget about your doubts and worries and act by faith, strengthen your inner being and heal the negative tensions that keep you chained down from reaching new heights.

"If you change the way you look at things, the things you look at change."-Wayne Dyer

Perfecting the pure positive state

Becoming perfect in positivity is a state of purity and should be our top priority in attainment. When someone reaches this state it is pure bliss as well as pure gain. One must come to realize that to gain is our higher purpose and to lose is our lower state of mind. By becoming perfect in our mission of attainment we are aligning with our highest point of self perfection. I encourage everyone to strive for this state of being and to do whatever it takes to reach it.

By attaining purity we then become pure as people on all levels of being. When we gain purity through positivity we are healed completely and we become one with our higher selves and potential. All the statements and ideas in this book have all boiled down to this one section. My goal is to create a transformation within people and to change their thinking and lives through the power of positivity. Follow my ideas and universal laws and you will be bound to succeed as well as obtain a better more rewarding life.

For those who attain this state you are truly blessed and will forever be as long as you take my teachings to heart. Understand that this state of mind and being is our highest possible attainment and that obtaining this position is the best thing that you could possibly do. Keep hard at work on your mission to purify and heal your old negative ways. Forget about your old ways for they are your worst enemy and will only lead you astray from your higher potential that shines within the heart of pure positivity. Reach for the stars and don't let anything or anyone bring you down. Stay strong and keep your head held up high, for this is the path to perfection. Becoming perfect in positivity is what we all want, so don't be afraid reach out and grab it, live it and love it.

"Positive purity is the answer to negative emptiness"

The new awakening and consciousness

A new awakening has been prophesized and I believe that this new awakening is a positive awakening. An awakening of the positive spirit within people, in order to change the world in a positive way. This kind of positive awakening and action will eventually get worked into the framework of our minds. Positivity will over power negativity a million to one. Negative people will be blown away by the impact of such positive power and change and will be likely transformed into a positive lifestyle change also.

This new conscious awakening takes motivation and action. If we do not act on our new awakening we will never truly gain its rewards. Although I'm sure that once we notice the truth about the higher power of the universe we will all bow down to it and surrender to its glory. Positivity is law and law is power, it is the higher knowingness that we must all submit to in order to live life to the fullest. The longer we hold back from surrendering ourselves to this higher positive power the longer we will be held back from our higher potential.

A positively powered world will run much smoother and will be much more responsive to positive change and production. We will think in a new way and a creative way. We must free our shallow minds from our controlled and conditioned negative reality. People don't deserve to suffer and live our shallow enforced lives. The truth is out and we must respond to its signals, for they are a plea for hope. We live under one world as one collective system, if we want positive change, there must be positive action first.

What are we waiting for go out there and speak your mind, and protest for what you believe in. Fight for your freedom and truth of positive rights and change. Create a new world, there is a need for a new world order, but not like people describe it as. We all think that the new world order is a terrible thing that we all dread, what is all of this crazy talk? What we need is a positive new world order, a world of open heartedness and generosity. In order to obtain a positive new world order we must be open to the idea of mass change. Our governments must let down their walls of hate, closed mindedness and denial of positive change. I encourage all people to get their ideas out there and let their hearts flood out into every corner of the world. There must be something we can do to help, I say let's send ship loads of people to help in third nations. The key to a working positive environment is to do unto others as you'd like them to do unto you. Help out others and they will likely help you (team work).

There must be incentive to help our harsh society; we must be willing to help in order to obtain change. Without the will to change and help for a personal, social and global change nothing will be done. If no one wants positive change we will continue to live our shadowed lives and be victims to our own insanity. We must ask ourselves why is there so many problems in the world today? Why is no one doing anything to change? Why are we so careless and stubborn? Is there hope for a better today and a better future I believe so and so should you. Once there is the belief/ realization that there is need for change; then we will be prepared to work towards our global cause together for the good of all.

"Act as if what you do makes a difference. It does. -William James

Positive solidity

1. The quality or state of being firm or strong in structure.

2. The quality of being substantial or reliable in character.

3. The condition or property of being solid. Soundness of mind, moral character, firm in yourself and decisions. Being solid in your positive beliefs is being stern and confident in your beliefs and actions. When a person achieves solidity they achieve peace of mind and gain confidence in their selves and their actions. These attributes are more than necessary and are extremely self improving. Find solidity within your new positive views and beliefs on life and lifestyle. Calm your mind by healing its negative

tendencies, and old ways of randomness and immorality. Be firm in your beliefs and actions and be solid in body, soul and mind. Become positive solidity and don't let anyone crack your hard cover shell with their negativity. Be better than the people that try to bring you down and rise above any limits they could even think of reaching. This is the art of positive solidity, and I encourage you to meditate on the idea and reach a state of positive solidity and free yourself from your thoughts. By becoming solid in pure positivity we become firm in our overall character, and this is the goal of becoming positively solid.

"Everything you do can be done better from a place of relaxation."
- Stephen C. Paul

Becoming/being a positive warrior

Being a positive warrior means to stand up for positive means and to fight off negativity. There is more to life than to simply live for our positive beliefs but to fight for them till death if necessary. Take the story of Jesus for instance Jesus stood firm to his beliefs and words until he had gotten crucified on the cross. He may have died but at least he died true to his beliefs and word. It is better to die true than to die a liar to yourself, others and the world around you.

Find your truth and stick with it until the end or until you are proven otherwise. Fight off negative distractions, and be firm in your actions. Positivity is the law and it deserves justice. Seek out your justice and make it a reality, shun those who enforce their negative judgment and actions upon you. Be better than the negative scum of the earth, enforce positivity and its truth/ power. Show the world that positivity is the higher power of the universe and that it is righteous and deserves respect.

Fight for your positive rights and freedoms, and fight to destroy of negative forces. The less negative force the better off the world is; so don't have fear in your actions for they are just. Be confident in your beliefs and find power within them and show others that same power that you have found. Show the world what positivity can do, and the benefits that it carries with it. Positivity is our sword and shield to protect us as we fight off negative energy in all forms. Be strong in mind and heart for they will help you in your life journey as a positive warrior. Trust in your higher potential, and power. Know yourself and stay true to yourself at all times. Don't let negativity try to destroy and or degrade your potential; fight for your positive potential no matter what.

"Your work is to discover your work and then with all your heart to give yourself to it." *- Buddha*

Positive tact/Consideration of others and circumstances (selflessness)

A major factor on our path to a positive life is to be aware of others and their needs. We must be almost selfless in our endeavors. If we seek personal happiness, we must also strive towards the happiness of others. Others have an impact on our lives that affect us; therefore we must be aware of this fact and act on it.

When considering the lives of others it is important to think of the effects of your actions and reactions. We must be mindful of knowing when, where and why to talk and act a certain way. We must become aware of others positive needs and wants. Everyone indulges in the positive endeavors and joys of life. We must become aware of the fact that we all are after the same thing; and that is good things.

Consider the fact that your actions have an impact on others lives. Be aware of karma and how it works in your social life and friendships. Be kind hearted and don't be afraid to spread the glory of positivity across your community. The more respect, love and positivity we give the more we will likely receive. Plot out positive actions and you will likely be bound to receive positive reactions.

It is important that we strive to give the respect to others that we expect to receive. Our actions are in a sense mirrored back to us. If we send negativity to others, we will be likely to receive negativity back. Although some people will be kind enough to let your negativity slip and we should learn from this kindness. We must grow out of our negative functioning's and treat others how we'd like to be treated (or better).

When we reach out to others, they will likely slowly grow comfortable and reach back. We've all shed tears, been hurt, struggled, been put down and mistreated. It's time to flee from the dark, cold void of negativity and stand up for a more righteous and rewarding cause. We must connect and correlate with each other and share our joy with others and let it be spread. Our shallow hearts are a disease that leads to more disease and infection.

I encourage people to strive towards putting an end to their negative behavior. We all grow and prosper in positivity, and we can all be healed by its power. Some people are so shallow minded to see what kind of damage their negativity is doing. Negativity will only hurt us as well as others emotionally, mentally and physically. When will we have the courage to rise against our collective negative tendencies? And what would our lives and the world be like without all of that collective negativity? Try asking yourselves these questions, and try to find an answer. Then try to imagine your life without any negativity, and how great it feels to be free from the shackles of all that negativity. We don't deserve to be engulfed in this negativity. We deserve the best; so I encourage everyone to join in and take part in helping our collective cause for the betterment of the world and its people.

"One should treat others as one would like others to treat oneself"

The importance of love and caring

Love and positivity is the fabric that binds us together. What would the world be without love? Without love we are left cold hearted and empty. We could all use someone who cares about us in our lives. There is no better feeling in the world than being loved and cared about. When we love one another with a pure heart we are connected in a special way. Love is understanding and accepting.

Love makes us addicted to caring, and it also has powerful reaction on people. When someone ridicules something we love, we tend to get very offended. Try asking yourself what you love? What would you do for what you love? And what lengths would you go to protect that love?

Try applying more love into your life, and watch as it changes how you feel. Love is a powerful feeling that makes us feel good about ourselves and the world around us. When we care about ourselves and others, we are more receptive to positive feedback. When we are in love we are willing to fight for that love, making us strong headed and hearted. Love life, love others and love the world around you, and protect that love at any cost.

"Love will keep us together"- *Captain & Tennille*

Using your positivity intelligently

Positivity is a necessity but using it intelligently is the back bone to positivity, and living a positive life. It is important that we be intelligent on how we use our positivity. If we are not intelligent in our endeavors we will easily fall into stupidity which is an aspect of negativity. We must know how to use our positivity in a way that will allow us to achieve our maximum positive potential.

Without an intelligent mindset we could not achieve our positive lifestyle. We must watch how we speak, act and think. Being intelligent means that we are thinking in a positive and productive nature as often as possible. Our thinking represents ourselves and our intentions. In order to achieve a positive lifestyle we must first have an intelligent approach to our intentions.

When we master being intelligent in our actions and decisions we gain control of our own destinies. The next step to positive intelligence is not only being intelligent, but to follow through with our positive intelligence and playing it out into action. Just as we blue print a house before building it, or write a script before a movie; we must also plan out our actions and ideas.

Positive intelligence will lead us into a life of organization and will act as our blue print for success. Without our intelligence we will be bound to live in our own stupidity. Choose to be smart in your choice and endeavors, because no one is responsible for them but you. Use your intelligence to your own advantage, and rise above your own negativity with your own intelligence. Notice how stupid you've been about your own positivity and fix it. This is your life and it is your decision to change your ways for a more positive and intelligent life.

"Knowledge is power"

Confidence in your positivity/ positivity in general

If we don't have confidence in positivity then we must reconsider why we would even live by it. For a person to reach their max potential they must have confidence in their selves and actions. First of all one must realize that they seek positive change, and healing in their own lives and that they indeed wish to live righteously. Being confident in our positivity is to have confidence in our higher selves and purpose.

When we are confident in our actions and selves we are more easily enabled to succeed. Believe in righteousness and a positive cause and thrive off of your success and gains. Thrive off of your over confidence and power, and encourage others to thrive as well. Be confident in your dreams and be confident in achieving them. Without confidence we are weak and vulnerable to failure.

Confidence takes awhile to build up but it is so worth the while. Practice being more confident and discover the feeling of joy that it brings to you. Once you realize that having as much confidence as you can possibly attain is a good thing to do, you will likely grow more and more confident with time and practice. Keep a strong head and heart and be confident with positivity. Know that positivity is truth, and through it is true power. Find confidence within this power and attain it and watch as it helps to work wonders in your life one day and one moment at a time.

"Confidence is the belief that you can achieve anything you put your mind to"

How our internal system and beliefs make up our actions which make up our self reflection

If we believe that we are our thoughts we are plunged into a world of being lost within the void of repetitive thinking whether positive or negative. When we relax and find ourselves behind the curtain of thought our true identities are found. We have been brainwashed by materiality and we lose sight of our true identities. Our true identities lie in being still, in control and structured strongly.

One of the most important things in our lives is to have positive beliefs. If we don't have positive beliefs then our selves, lives and reflection of self to other is tainted because our beliefs are negative. "What we believe becomes reality". This is why people around the world are crazy and it's because they believe in crazy ideas and things. Our minds are miraculous as well as tricky.

We become who we believe ourselves to be, and we achieve what we believe we can achieve. If we believe that we are cool people then we will tend to act like cool people therefore giving off the vibe of being cool. Our minds pick up on our beliefs and feelings about them. If we have negative beliefs then were going to feel bad about them. For example little Timmy thinks that he's a loser because all the kids at school think so. What is the point of making yourself an even bigger loser by letting yourself think that you're a loser as well as getting treated like one? It doesn't help you to believe in negative thoughts and beliefs about yourself.

When we realize the fact that our personal beliefs make up our ideas of self and structure; our internal and external self reflection we'll be bound to change. Those who believe that they can be set free from their negative entrapment and self punishment will. Those that don't have enough self faith will perish within it for as long as it stays real within their belief systems and thought systems.

Our personal development relies on our own personal positive belief system as well as a strongly structured self image along with as many positive traits as possible. Our personalities should be comforting and personally satisfying on a personal level. Discover what is right for you and what feels comfortable.

If we seek to change our attributes we should look at ourselves from a mental perspective. A perspective of positive and personal self creation; almost like creating a character on a video game. We can choose our own styles and we can create a statement of our own creativity and individuality. Why be boring with your style, go create something that shines you. Express yourself and passion through your looks and character as a total bundle. Create the you that you wish to achieve.

It is important to be well developed in positive traits and attributes that will allow you to succeed. Although it is also very important to find yourself and the person you want to be and to deeply try to connect on that level. Some people wish to be beautiful but they don't do anything to become beautiful. We are all dreamers yet we don't always put our dreams into action.

It is time to wake up and put your dreams into action and to become the best you; you can be. We must be aware of not only what makes us happy but also successful in many areas. There must be a balance of work and play and we must be able to deal with our circumstances. If we are not able to juggle the events of our lives we could get very unorganized and stressed. A smart individual would plan out their actions to a successful life. The people that don't tend to plan ahead tend to sometimes stream behind the people that do.

"Create the you that you wish to achieve"

Realizing the potential of your creativity/imagination and applying your personal creativity for positive results

Within all of us lies the tremendous energy of our minds which has the potential to be extremely creative in some people. Some people realize the potential that their personal imaginations have in our modern evolving world. Our ideas have the ability to change the world and the people on it as well. All the books, art, structure, inventions and ideas came from modern day thinkers. People who thought about things in a very in depth way tend to figure them out.

This theory of realization by thinking has been awed upon forever; our minds and selves need to grow as well as learn. The more we learn and expand our consciousness/ thinking the more good/ useful ideas that we will have gained. By having a positive mental attitude and focusing on solving problems and creating new ideas the better off in our society we are.

It is important like I've continuously stated that we have control over our thoughts and imaginations. To be in a lucid state of being and being aware of our thoughts and ideas so that we can properly use them and apply them to and into our lives. If we snooze we lose because there is nothing to remember if we are too un attentive to receive and store information. This is why we should always have a notebook handy so that we can jot down our ideas daily, so that we can use them at one point. Our creativity will open up door ways for our success and will expand our consciousness and thinking broadening our possibilities.

"Open your mind and live the life of your dreams"

List of positive skills, attributes and characteristics that could help you and strengthen your character

- Confidence

- Happiness

- Conversation skills

- Work skills

- Organization

- Leadership skills

- Relationship skills

- Strong heartedness

- Persistence

- Strength

- Pride

- Faith/hope

- Loving

- Intelligent

- Recreational skills

- Teamwork

- Cleanliness

- Problem solving skills

- Maintenance skills

- Innovation skills

- Personal development skills

- Observational skills

- Creativity

- Peacefulness

- Control

- Determination

- Responsible

Positivism and religion

Many people are confused about religion including myself. Religion is a very confusing thing for it doesn't have much fact to back it. On the other hand many religions teach the power of good over evil such as Christianity. Positivity is based on facts and it is a belief system within itself, therefore it can very well be a religion. Positivity is whatever works for you in a positive way whether it is spirituality, physical things or mental aspects.

Positivity is open to new ideas as long as it has a positive contribution to your life, society and the life of others. As long as we are positive our problems will melt away whether physical, mental or spiritual problems. Positivism teaches that whatever you want in life u should be happy and feeling good about it. What more could you ask for in a religion.

The thing about Positivism is that it can conjoin with most all other religions in a beneficial way. It is a religion that enhances all other religions whether it is Christianity, Buddhist, Wiccan, Muslim, Islam, Judaism or whatever. Now the key aspect of most religion is gods or gods. Most religions God or gods are depicted as angelic and good with positive and loving aspect, unless they are evil gods. The main the thing is that anyone seeking a positive and loving god believes in positivism. If you believe in positivism then why not practice its teachings and live faithful to them.

Positivism is a religion within itself whether physical, spiritual or both it's really up to you and a person's personal preference. Our minds are programmed by us to believe in whatever we want; so go ahead be free to decide what's true for you. Don't let anyone tell you what's wrong or right without your consent, make your own decisions and stay true to your personal truth. I only suggest positivity as a personal life experience and lesson that I have made for myself. You can either choose to listen to what I have to say or you can turn it down, put the book down and walk away from its teaching, but I think that everyone and all of society can grow and gain from its teachings. The road of negativity is a road of hell and to hell; follow me my people into a new revolution a revolution of light, truth, justice, growth, happiness and prosperity.

"Positivism does neither support nor turn down the aspects or beliefs of any religion but positivism in general"

Positive, negative and neutral personality types and the importance of the positive state (pure plus)

Personality types and Mind states:

-Pure positive intentional people-"pure plus"

-Positive people with some negative intention

-Pure neutral people who don't really have much of any intention

-Pure negative intentional people

-Neutral with either positive or negative or a mixture

-Negative people with some positive intention

There are only 3 pure states although the pure positive state is the best state because it makes the best use out of everything. It is the only state that is really true and compassionate. It is a transformative state that wishes to change all other states into pure positivity. It takes negative energy and makes it into a positive energy, it takes a neutral energy and it turns it into useful positive energy.

Neutral and negative energy is stupid and degrading. Why must we have to face each other with the chance of failure and destruction available? Why must there be hatred and un- acceptance? The answer is that there are people who run on the mind state and personality type of negative intentions. These people are un- pure and are destructive to not only themselves but their community.

When we run on the personality type and mind state of a purely positive person with positive intention, we are becoming positive role models for ourselves and the people around us everyday. These people are the people who make all the difference. These are the people that are true and can be trusted. The others are only fakes and knock offs that will stab you in the back when possible.

I like to call the pure positive state of people "pure plus". I like to repeat this to myself in my head or out loud. The words "pure plus" I find to actually draw us into that state faster. Also if you are being tempted by negativity in anyway, just repeat the words "pure plus" and you will be filled with the power within positivity. It will fill you with wisdom, knowledge, power and guidance to do the right thing at all times. Anyone who attains this state of "pure positivity/ pure plus" is bound to change themselves, their community and possibly even the world. It is positive people who are happy and are finding enlightenment, not the negative people.

So what have you got to lose? Find the "pure plus" within yourself and let its light shine upon the world and others. Be proud of you for being able to conquer evil and negative intention. Doing so can be a very difficult task so if you can escape your own negative tendencies as well as being able to ignore and dilute of the worlds negativity; then give yourself a round of applause because you truly are a star and will be known as someone who actually had an impact on the world.

"The cup can either be seen as half empty or half full, yet I see the cup as completely full"

Concluding thoughts:

After finishing this book and meditating upon its ideas and watching how they have changed my life it's really astonishing. I am in eternal awe of the power within positivity. I have went from being homeless, jobless and addicted to drugs and alcohol to working full time and holding down a place, as well as my longest relationship. I feel that my life would never change if I hadn't changed myself I could have fell into a downward spiral, yet I kept my head up and stayed strong. I had faith in myself and my beliefs and I have come to write and publish my very first book at age 21.

I still see negativity around me in my everyday life but I don't establish myself with it. I do what I need to keep my positive lifestyle, and I have gained a feeling of great authority from this. I change people's lives daily, because I actually care. All my care comes from my knowledge of positive power, as well as all my happiness, strength and honor. The more I honor positivity the more strengthened I am by its glory and power. My life as well as I becomes an expression of my honor. People pick up on this and begin to wonder why I am so happy? Why I am so nice? Why I am so helpful and considerate and respectable? The answer is my beliefs towards positivity and my feelings that come with that understanding. It is truly blissful to experience this feeling of pure positivity and bliss/ harmony. I have found my enlightenment and my meaning, and I want to share it with you. It is has become more than a symbol for me it has become my religion, my lifestyle, myself and my beliefs. I would do anything to hold this truth close to my heart and never let go for the world.

I only hope that I can change the lives of others, for a brighter today and a brighter future. I would like to thank everyone who took the time to read it and I promise that you will be satisfied with the results this book will bring to your life. Although these things don't just come, they must be worked upon, as well as into your mind and soul.

"We must become the change that we seek to obtain".

Thank you to **everyone** and **everything**
that put meaning into this world,

thank you to **my girlfriend** who's been there
for me through the toughest of times,

and thank you to **my family** for being there,

thank you to **everyone at Trafford publishing** for
working hard with me to complete this book,

and thanks to the **universe** for mothering me and giving
me the opportunity to be alive, free and happy!